The A.R.T. of Balance™

A Three-Step Strategy for Busy, Burned Out
Executives Who Want to Have It All

BY

Dr. RJ Verwayne

Printed in the United States of America

ISBN: 978-0-578-73938-0

Dedication

To God, for entrusting me with this vision and guiding me through every step. Thank you for shining the light on me when I'm in a hiding place. I'm in awe of your grace.

To my talented, busy, and exhausted clients, whose journeys inspired this work and whose determination to find balance fuels my passion.

To my husband Adrian, and my children, Adriana and Ryan who are my constant motivators and reminders of the importance of maintaining balance in my own life.

To Marquel Russell and Aundrae Gaskin for shaping me into an unstoppable business owner who actively transforms lives, directly and indirectly, every day.

And to my family and friends, who cheer me on and expect nothing but greatness from me—your unwavering support means everything.

To my momma Sheneal whose lioness-like strength and pride activates my never-ending audaciousness.

Thank you all for being the pillars of my strength and the sources of my inspiration.

This book is for you.

Table of Contents

[INTENTIONALLY LEFT BLANK]

Foreword

The A.R.T. of Balance is a groundbreaking approach for busy executives to flourish in both their personal and professional lives. Dr. RJ's teaching of authenticity, relentless rest, and time consciousness challenged executives like me to devise approaches that require you to place the mirror in your face and make the necessary adjustments for the ultimate success. I remember speaking with Dr. RJ about how this strategy can be implemented with other legal experts across the nation and how the balance of it all is necessary for this niche field of high performers.

In 2014, I was originally introduced to Dr. RJ as the proclaimed clinical director of a counseling agency. From that moment until now, I knew that barriers would be broken once Dr. Johnson unleashed her talent to the world. Fast forward to late 2022 as I was going through massive waves of high functioning perfectionism while serving elected officials, I began to research how I could be most effective to both my team and those high performing officials that I served. Going through Dr. RJ's Executive Burnout curriculum has proved that you must tackle the ROOT of why you tend to crash and burn. Using her philosophy "sprint-rest" has helped me as a high performer to center self-care and make that a priority in my life.

If you are seeking to have work-life balance, increase your rest to maximize your performance or if you just want to add tactics to your life that help you overcome persistent feelings of pure exhaustion, this book is for you. Enlisting this roadmap of strategies will elevate your life and provide a balanced approach to your success.

Congratulations on your latest gift to the rest of us. Your continued pursuit to provide top tier, high performers with the tools leading to our success is the proof that your journey is never-ending and that you are the true gift to all.

LeNora Hawkins
LeNora Hawkins
Chief Administrative Officer and a
Student thriving from The A.R.T. of Balance™

Acknowledgments

To the busy and overwhelmed executives who served as my inspiration, thank you for fueling my passion to create this work. Without your experiences and challenges, this book would not have come to life. Your journeys have continually motivated me to pursue this project with dedication and purpose.

To the supporters listed below, thank you for your enthusiastic and unwavering support and for sharing your thoughts on balance. It matters.

LeNora Hawkins- "Curating a balanced life is the key to success!"

Christal Brown- "Balance is important because it helps me measure the growth and authenticity of my vision."

Eugene Burke- "Balance sets the tone for what needs to be done."

Lekesha Smith- "Authenticity is indeed a superpower."

Bilal Fladger- "Balance is a foundational component for our family to strive individually and collectively."

Gail Jackson- "Balance will help me with saying no to things requested of me."

Kala Walton-"Balance brings me peace."

Vernessa Glover- "Balance helps to anchor priorities and find and keep peace."

Melissa Jones- "Balance ensures stability, well-being, and harmony in life."

Josina Woodruff- "Balance is crucial for realizing my true potential, not only for myself but for my family and the communities I serve."

INTRODUCTION

Welcome to The A.R.T. of Balance—a strategy especially designed for the six and seven-figure CEOs, corporate leaders, and high-level executives who excel in their fields but find themselves overwhelmed by the constant demands of their roles. I'm Dr. Raushannah Johnson Verwayne, a licensed clinical psychologist specializing in helping high performers like you achieve a balanced and fulfilling life.

You've built an impressive career, enjoy financial success, have your version of a picture-perfect family, and can go on a vacation whenever you please. Yet, despite these life luxuries, you may find yourself struggling with burnout, anxiety, and stress. The pressure of constantly making decisions and maintaining your success can feel like juggling too many balls at once, with the fear that dropping one will cause everything to collapse.

This book is for you if you've reached a level of success that few understand or if you're on the path toward a similar goal. You've achieved your dreams, yet you don't feel the joy you expected. Instead, you're burning the candle at both ends, feeling the immense pressure to keep everything together.

Why This Book?

In my years of working with high-level professionals, I've discovered a common thread among those at the top—they often lack the support they need. When you're the best at what you do, people assume you have it all figured out. But even the most successful people need balance, rest, and time management to sustain their achievements and well-being.

This book introduces you to "The Art of Balance," a simple yet effective three-step system that has transformed individuals and organizations. I developed this concept after working with thousands of professionals who, despite their success, felt overwhelmed and stressed. This strategy focuses on authenticity, relentless rest, and time consciousness and is designed to help you rediscover yourself, prioritize rest, and manage your time effectively to truly have it all just the way you want.

The Modern Dilemma of Burnout

Burnout is not a new phenomenon; however, remote work and digital captivity have shaped the concept of burnout into an ugly, costly monster of an issue.

The term "work-life balance" has received a lot of attention in the past few years, so much so that there are spinoffs. You've likely heard or even used one of the following terms: work-life harmony, work-life flow, work-life fit, work-life integration, etc. Balance in this case does not mean perfect and equal parts or an equal distribution of weight. It means constant calibration or slight adjustments in order to create a life that you actually love. Consider these synonyms of balance; composure, poise, stability, and steadiness, as you read this book and implement the strategies. I should let you know that this book is amazing, and you'll finish it quickly. Once you do, no worries there's more. Go to bonus.artofbalancebook.com for access to the A.R.T. of Balance™ online course.

How This Book Can Help

If you read Executive Burnout: 7 Reasons Why High Performers Crash and Burn Before Reaching Their Full Potential, you already know that my writing style is all about simplicity and immediate implementation. The conversational style is intentional. I love to read, and my favorite books are short, sweet, and to the point with transformational take-aways. That's what you'll find here in The A.R.T. of Balance: A Three-Step Strategy for Busy, Burned-Out Professionals Who Want to Have it All. The book is divided into three sections, each with real-life examples of the work-life balance dilemma. I carefully selected the executives in hopes that you might see yourself in at least one of the scenarios, particularly because high achievers often experience loneliness and shame when confronting inner thoughts and feelings. Trust me, you're not the only one who has felt that way whatever it is. You will also find experiential exercises called The Balance Blueprint which will accelerate your learning on the journey to balance.

By the time you have finished reading this book, you will be able to immediately make meaningful changes in your daily life. Now, I know from experience that some of you will get overwhelmed by trying to make all of the changes at once. Pace yourself. Make one change per month, practice, make it a habit, then move on to the next task. Once you've mastered a task, reward yourself by checking it off of your list. Nothing feels better than saying "done, what's next?" with confidence. The goal is to change at a rate of 1% each day and these exercises will enhance the process. To get started you'll need a calendar and a journal, both of which you can find at bonus.theartofbalancebook.com as a complimentary gift.

In Real Life

One of my roles as a clinical psychologist is to train high-performing professionals on how to achieve balance. In a room full of executives from different parts of the country, all nodding their heads in unison to cultural references and shared experiences I asked "Where are you from, Dr. Rosen?".

"California," she replied.

"What about you Jeff?"

"Ohio".

"And you Brianna?"

"I'm a Georgia Peach from the real Atlanta".

The conversation quickly turned to how we all, despite our diverse backgrounds and upbringing, had similar subconscious beliefs about work and success.

"Programming, we grew up hearing certain messages about work and success," someone said.

"Money doesn't grow on trees," Will said.

Shade added, "You have to work twice as hard just to be in the room."

Another voice in the room echoed, "A man that don't work, don't eat."

I curiously inquired, "But what about messages concerning rest and balance?"

"No!" the room collectively and loudly responded. In sum, "Get a good education and work hard" was the extent of the wisdom imparted to them. Nothing about balance, rest, or mental health. Until now.

I then asked everyone to list the roles they play in their lives. "Mom, sister, aunt, family banker, family planner, scheduler, relationship manager, prayer warrior," the lists went on. Many had ten, fifteen, or even twenty roles. The exercise highlighted the sheer number of responsibilities we juggle daily, often without conscious awareness.

I shared that not even I was exempt from the subconscious programming that the only path to success was the Overwork Blvd. After licensure, I became a clinical director at a large mental health agency in Atlanta. At age twenty-eight, which was fairly young for the role, I felt the need to prove myself constantly. Picture me at 5 feet and 3 and a half inches, with a youthful face, and a pencil skirt, pearls, and heels to make myself feel "professional", I overworked to demonstrate that I belonged. Even after having children, I continued the relentless grind, missing out on important family moments and justifying my behavior under the guise of hustle culture.

About four years later, my husband suggested I start my own private practice. I planned everything meticulously—no traffic, close to home, daycare nearby. Yet, I found myself overworking again, often sleeping in my office despite living five minutes away. The lack of balance and perpetual burnout were issues from within. While sitting at my desk at 2 am busy doing nothing, it finally dawned on me. "It's an inside job".

This epiphany led me to develop "the art of balance." I had to be aware that the problem was internal. Balance and burnout are inside jobs. They aren't primarily the fault of external factors like employers or even societal expectations. They stem from within us.

In this room of highly skilled C-suite executives, I knew that our roundtable discussion during the second half of the training would be challenging. It began with a four-word question from Tangie, "Ok, so now what?"

Tangie is a powerhouse in the accounting world. In her mid-forties, married for about eight years, she embraces life through travel, social engagements with friends, and cherished moments with her sorority sisters. Professionally, Tangie holds a significant role as a partner at a large public accounting firm. Her expertise lies in conducting audits for Fortune 500 companies, ensuring financial accuracy and integrity.

In Tangie's own words, she's "where the buck stops." She's responsible for the quality execution of audits, ensuring that investors—from those putting in $20 to those with millions in the market—can trust the financial statements of these massive companies. Tangie oversees international teams, engages closely with C-suite executives, and navigates the intense pressures and tight timelines that come with regulatory compliance and client demands.

When an audit is in full swing, Tangie's days are packed with meetings. She checks in with her team to ensure everything is on track and that no issues are overlooked. Her interactions are not limited to her team; she also meets with clients to foster relationships and make sure they feel confident in the auditing process. Each company's unique culture and systems require Tangie to tailor her team's approach accordingly.

Besides meetings, Tangie reviews the audit work, focusing on high-risk areas to ensure standards are met. If issues arise, she steps in to guide her team and resolve problems. This intense schedule is just a "normal day" for Tangie; unforeseen challenges only add to the complexity.

Tangie's role requires substantial travel, both domestic and international. In any given two-week period, she might visit multiple cities, including international destinations. This travel is crucial for maintaining client relationships and overseeing her global teams, though it can be exhausting.

Despite her demanding career, Tangie is deeply committed to her personal life. Her husband, who also travels frequently and runs his own business, shares the challenge of balancing work and home life. They have a dog, adding another layer of responsibility, especially when their schedules get hectic.

Tangie also plays a significant role in her extended family. Being the most successful in her career among her siblings, she feels the pressure to guide her nieces and nephews in their educational and career paths. This sense of duty extends to her sorority sisters and their children, who know they can rely on "Auntie Tangie" for support and advice.

Her parents, who are still alive, are another source of responsibility. Tangie anticipates that she will need to contribute to their long-term care as they age, adding to the list of roles she juggles daily.

Balancing these responsibilities is a continual challenge for Tangie. She admits that sometimes she excels at it, while other times she struggles. A significant turning point was taking a twelve-week masterclass on executive burnout, which provided her with tools and strategies to manage stress and find balance. We'll talk more about Tangie later. But first, I have a quick assignment for you. Set a timer for 15 minutes and without thinking too hard, write what your dream life would look like, then visualize it. You can find a template at bonus.artofbalancebook.com.

Section One

AUTHENTICITY

"You are a masterpiece. Act like it."-Dr. RJ

Authenticity in Real Life

I settled into my seat at the Commerce Club, notepad and pen ready. I was eager to discuss my latest book with Kelsey, a seasoned executive who had experienced burnout firsthand. The atmosphere with the muted conversations of professionals on their lunch breaks, created a backdrop of productivity and ambition.

I began by explaining the concept to Kelsey. "It's The Art of Balance. You know, The Art of Balance isn't new for me. I'm just putting words to it. It's going to be the second part of Executive Burnout. Executive Burnout is like the why, and now Art of Balance is like, okay, what do we do next? It'll be a three-step system, discussing authenticity, relentless rest, and time consciousness to prevent burnout. It's moving from the why to the what's next."

Kelsey nodded, signaling her understanding as I continued, "I want to get the manuscript done while everything is in my head so thank you for doing this so quickly."

"Okay, good," Kelsey replied, her tone supportive.

I leaned forward slightly, her curiosity piqued. "Alrighty. I don't have any official questions. I really just want to hear—well, let's start with what was your life like prior to working on balance?"

Kelsey sighed, her expression reflecting a mixture of exhaustion and relief. "Crazy. I was miserable. And this realization just hit me recently. I don't think I ever really spent time thinking about how others perceived me. But looking back, I think people saw me as this stressed-out person with all this craziness in her life."

"Mm-hmm," I murmured, prompting Kelsey to continue.

"And the downside of that is some people might still expect to see me that way. But when they see me responding differently, they're like, oh, something's changed," Kelsey explained.

"Did you...?" I started to ask, but Kelsey interjected.

"Somewhere along this process, I crossed that threshold of what I care about and what I don't. When you get to a place where you can display and speak about what you care about and what you don't, you know, you... I heard you use the word authenticity. I think authenticity is one of the things that comes out."

I smiled, impressed. "When did you decide, okay, I'm going to make an intentional decision to do things differently?"

Kelsey's eyes grew distant as she recalled, "I didn't have anything I wanted—no beautiful vacations, no fancy trips, no quality time with my girlfriends, cousins, or family. Sitting at home watching everyone else enjoy these things made me see, like, why don't you have it?"

"Mm-hmm. What are some of the things you did to go from being this person you really weren't to your authentic self?" I inquired.

"I did your workbook," Kelsey admitted with a chuckle. "You know how sometimes they say you have to hit rock bottom before you come up? That was me. I had just bottomed out. I was overwhelmed with not having the things I wanted. One major turning point was my health. Post-pandemic, around 2021 or 2022, I couldn't walk upstairs without breathing heavily."

"Mm-hmm," I nodded, listening intently.

"I didn't even know that person," Kelsey continued. "One morning, I saw a gym on Instagram. Nobody knew I was going; I wasn't even sure what time the class started. I woke up at 4:30 AM, drove there, and sat in the parking lot until someone showed up at 5:30. That day was a turning point for me. I kept asking myself why I was out of shape and why I wasn't taking care of myself. Everyone else had what they needed, but I needed help."

"Yeah," I responded softly.

"I felt a little crazy getting up so early and sitting in the parking lot, but once I worked out that one day, I went back every single day and lost about twenty-three, twenty-four pounds," Kelsey said, a proud smile spreading across her face.

"That's amazing," I praised. "Why do you think, I'll say black women in particular, why do you think we put everyone else before ourselves? What is it about us that makes us do that automatically?"

Kelsey sighed, pondering the question. "Oh, because we saw our mama and our grandmamma and our aunties do it. We were just told that the world expects us to handle business and take care of things. I also think a lot of us are jaded into believing that if we don't do it, no one else will. My Type A personality doesn't want things to appear as if they're falling apart."

"And if things are falling apart, what does that mean?" I probed.

"Oh, they think less of you, and they judge you. People treat you how they view you. If they think you're less than, they treat you like you're less than," Kelsey explained.

"It sounds like keeping things together is a survival tactic," I observed.

"Absolutely," Kelsey agreed. "Survival."

"Tell me about your authentic self now," I prompted.

Kelsey explained more about prioritizing her delayed foot surgery. "My authentic self now says, yeah, work is important, but I need my feet done. I need my surgery. Yes, I'm going to be out from April until July. This firm will keep working, but if my feet don't work, then I won't be working. When I come back, I'll pick up where I left off," Kelsey said, her voice firm and resolute.

"So being your authentic self means that you put your health and well-being first?" I clarified.

"Absolutely," Kelsey affirmed.

"Okay," I said, jotting down notes. "And what about the fear that taking care of oneself will reduce their ability to operate at a high level? Many of my clients worry about this."

Kelsey smiled, feeling validated and hopeful. "Thank you, Dr. RJ. It means a lot when the world sees you as someone with high regard for yourself, they honor it."

I smiled, jotting down notes. "You've come a long way, Kelsey. Your story will inspire many executives struggling with burnout to find their balance."

Authenticity Explained

Authenticity is defined as "the quality of being real; being actually or exactly what is claimed." To be authentic is to be clear about one's own most basic feelings, desires, and convictions, and to openly express one's stance in the public arena. (Nunes, 2021)

In a world that often values appearances over substance, being true to oneself is fundamental. For executives, this means understanding and aligning with your core values, both in your personal life and professional endeavors. The pressure to perform, to always be on, and to juggle a myriad of responsibilities can lead to burnout and a lack of balance.

You're a top executive, constantly on the move, always making decisions, perpetually in "go mode."

You're praised for your relentless work ethic and ability to get things done. But beneath that layer of high performance, there's often a nagging feeling of being stuck in an endless cycle of "doing" instead of "being." Sound familiar?

Imagine a life where your daily wins are acknowledged, where you journal morning and night, gaining deeper insight into yourself, how you view the world, and others around you. Picture setting boundaries and saying "no" without any guilt, establishing and maintaining a morning and night routine, and placing yourself at the top of your to-do list. This is not a dream–this can be your new reality. There is immense power within you, a power that we often fail to fully recognize. Your purpose is for the greater good but in order to fulfill it you must show up as the best version of yourself; rested, not burned out or stressed out, but ready to live life to the fullest.

It's nearly impossible to show up as the best version of yourself when you don't even know who that is. Authenticity starts with self-awareness.

Show Up and Show Out

In today's culture, we're bombarded with messages that glorify overworking. It's easy to fall into the trap of equating long hours with success. However, this mindset can lead to burnout, decreased productivity, and a strained work-life balance. Here's where journaling comes in as a game-changer.

To truly understand yourself, spend time alone and engage in introspection. One powerful tool for this is journaling.

The Hidden Benefits of Journaling

1. Increased Insight

Journaling acts as a mirror to your thoughts. When you put pen to paper, you gain a deeper understanding of your actions, motivations, and goals. It allows you to step back and analyze your experiences from a different perspective.

For instance, if you've had a challenging day dealing with a difficult situation at work, writing about it can help you see patterns you might have missed. Are there recurring themes in how you handle conflict? Are there particular triggers that set you off? Recognizing these patterns can provide valuable insights that inform better decision-making.

2. Provides Clarity

In the whirlwind of daily responsibilities, it's easy to lose sight of the bigger picture. Journaling helps you cut through the noise and focus on what's truly important. By regularly writing about your goals and priorities, you can declutter your mind and keep your vision clear.

Imagine starting your day by jotting down your top three priorities. This simple habit can bring tremendous clarity, ensuring that your actions align with your long-term objectives rather than getting lost in the minutiae.

3. Teaches You to Teach People How to Treat You

One of the most profound benefits of journaling is that it helps you understand your boundaries and how you want to be treated. When you reflect on interactions and relationships, you become more aware of what you will and won't tolerate.

For example, if you find that you're consistently overcommitting and feeling overwhelmed, journaling can help you recognize this pattern. You can then set clear boundaries and communicate them effectively, teaching others how to respect your time and energy.

Take a moment to explore different types of journals and choose one. You can start by downloading the free journal samples here:

Addressing Common Challenges

Doing Instead of Being

High-performing executives often struggle with the constant need to "do" rather than "be." The addiction to "doing" is often a learned behavior stemming from early messages of how to achieve success. Here's a reminder...you are already ENOUGH. Journaling provides a space for introspection, allowing you to cultivate a sense of presence and mindfulness. By regularly reflecting on your experiences, you can shift from a reactive state to a more proactive, intentional way of living.

Overworking Due to Cultural Messages

Cultural narratives and early childhood messages often glorify the hustle, making it challenging to break free from the cycle of overwork. Journaling helps you question these narratives and redefine what success means to you. Through regular self-reflection, you can detach from societal pressures and create a work-life balance that truly resonates with your values and your authentic self.

Struggle with Work-Life Balance

Finding a balance between work and personal life can be a constant battle for high-performing executives. Journaling allows you to gain perspective, assess your priorities, and make necessary changes to create a more harmonious lifestyle. By writing about your daily experiences and feelings, you can identify areas where you may need to adjust boundaries or re-evaluate priorities. Journaling is a superpower.

How to Get Started with Journaling

The beauty of journaling lies in its simplicity. Here are a few tips to get you started:

Set Aside Time: Dedicate a specific time each day for journaling. It could be in the morning to set the tone for your day or in the evening to reflect on your experiences. I personally journal for five minutes in the morning and five minutes at night.

Use Prompts: If you're unsure where to start, use prompts like "What am I grateful for today?" or "What challenges did I face, and how did I overcome them?"

Be Honest: Your journal is a judgment-free zone. Write honestly about your thoughts, feelings, and experiences without worrying about grammar or structure. If you're worried about your thoughts being discovered, no worries. Use a lock whether it's a password or a physical lock.

Review and Reflect: Periodically review your journal entries to identify patterns and gain deeper insights. Reflect on how your journaling practice has impacted your day-to-day life and most importantly, acknowledge and celebrate your progress.

Types of Journaling

There are various types of journaling, each offering unique insights:

Reflective Journaling: Write about your day, your thoughts, and your feelings. This helps you understand your emotional responses and thought patterns.

Gratitude Journaling: Focus on what you're thankful for. This shifts your mindset from what's lacking to what's abundant.

Goal-Oriented Journaling: Outline your objectives and track your progress. This keeps you aligned with your ambitions.

The Benefits of Different Types of Journaling
Journaling is a powerful tool that can offer numerous benefits depending on the type you choose to practice. Here, we explore the advantages of reflective journaling, gratitude journaling, and goal-oriented journaling.

Reflective Journaling

Reflective journaling involves writing about your experiences, thoughts, and feelings to gain insights and understanding.

1. Enhanced Self-Awareness

Reflective journaling helps you understand your emotions, triggers, and patterns of behavior. By regularly examining your thoughts, you become more aware of your inner workings, aiding in personal growth.

2. Improved Problem-Solving Skills

Writing about your challenges and reflecting on possible solutions can enhance your problem-solving abilities. It encourages critical thinking and helps you consider different perspectives.

3. Stress Reduction

Reflecting on your day and expressing your emotions through writing can be a therapeutic process. It allows you to release pent-up feelings, reducing stress and anxiety levels.

4. Better Decision-Making

Through reflection, you can analyze past decisions and their outcomes. This practice helps you make more informed choices in the future, leading to better decision-making skills.

Gratitude Journaling

Gratitude journaling focuses on writing about the things you are thankful for, which can shift your mindset and improve your overall well-being.

1. Increased Positivity

Regularly noting down things you are grateful for can shift your focus from negative to positive aspects of your life. This practice fosters a more optimistic outlook.

2. Enhanced Emotional Well-Being

Gratitude journaling can lead to higher levels of happiness and satisfaction. Acknowledging the good things in your life can boost your mood and overall emotional health.

3. Stronger Relationships

Expressing gratitude can improve your relationships. When you appreciate the people in your life and acknowledge their contributions, it strengthens your bonds and fosters mutual respect.

4. Reduced Stress

Focusing on gratitude can lower stress levels by helping you concentrate on what you have rather than what you lack. This shift can bring a sense of peace and contentment.

Goal-Oriented Journaling

Goal-oriented journaling involves writing about your ambitions, creating action plans, and tracking your progress toward achieving your goals.

1. Clearer Focus

Writing down your goals helps clarify what you want to achieve. Detailed documentation of your objectives provides a clear roadmap, making it easier to stay focused and committed.

2. Increased Motivation

Regularly reviewing your goals and tracking your progress can boost motivation. Seeing how far you've come can inspire you to keep moving forward and maintain momentum.

3. Enhanced Accountability
Goal-oriented journaling holds you accountable for your actions. By setting deadlines and milestones, you are more likely to stay on track and achieve your targets.

4. Personal Growth
Setting and working towards goals encourages continuous self-improvement. This type of journaling helps you identify areas for development and fosters a growth mindset.

Incorporating any of these journaling practices into your daily routine can yield significant benefits, enhancing various aspects of your personal and professional life. Start experimenting with different types to find the one that resonates most with you! I like them all but gratitude journaling gives me the best results, probably because it's quick and easy to maintain.

By journaling regularly, you gain insights into your emotions, strengths, and areas for improvement. This self-awareness allows you to show up authentically in every aspect of your life. When you understand yourself, it empowers you to teach others how to treat you.

Have you selected and downloaded your free journal yet?

Just Say No

The Importance of Boundaries

One of the most challenging aspects of executive life and life in general is learning to say no. I could probably write another book on this topic alone. Stay tuned. However, setting boundaries is essential for maintaining balance and protecting your mental health.

Setting boundaries and learning to say no are essential for maintaining a balanced life. Without these limits, we risk overcommitting, leading to unnecessary stress and burnout. Boundaries help protect our time and energy, ensuring we can focus on what truly matters to us—whether it's personal aspirations, family, or self-care. By saying no to activities or demands that do not align with our priorities, we create space for growth and well-being, ultimately achieving a more fulfilling and harmonious life.

Ways to Say No

Here are different ways to assertively and respectfully decline additional responsibilities without damaging relationships (although in my mind I want to just tell you to get somebody else to do it):

The Direct No:

"I appreciate the offer, but I'm going to have to pass this time."

The Delayed No:

"Can I get back to you on that? I need to check my schedule."

The Conditional No:

"I can't do that, but I can help with something else."

The Delegated No:

"I'm not available, but perhaps [Name] can assist you."

The Compassionate No:

"I appreciate you thinking of me. I don't have the bandwidth to give you the 100% that you deserve, so I have to pass. Please keep checking in."

The Absolute No:
"No."

Learning to say no helps you protect your time and energy, allowing you to focus on what truly matters. It also reinforces your authenticity by aligning your actions with your core values and priorities.

Balance Blueprint: Take a moment to think about the last time you actually said "no". How did you feel? Where in your body did you feel it? Was there any guilt involved? Now, write about it. Yes, right now, right here.

Self-Mastery

The Discipline of Self-Love

Discipline is often misunderstood as a form of self-punishment, but in reality, it is the highest form of self-love. Discipline involves making choices that are in your best interest, even when they are difficult. And guess what, discipline is more effective than motivation. Motivation is finicky but discipline is a sure thing.

Practicing Discipline

Here are some ways to cultivate discipline in your life:

Create a Routine

Establish a daily schedule that includes time for work, rest, and personal interests. Consistency builds habits. Focus on what MUST be done and keep it simple.

Set Goals

Define clear, achievable goals. Break them down into smaller, manageable tasks. Resist the urge to get everything done at once. Slowly and deliberately is the key.

Prioritize Self-Care

Make time for activities that rejuvenate you, whether it's exercise, reading, or spending time with loved ones. Self-care isn't selfish. Caring for yourself allows you to show up as the best version of yourself for others.

Hold Yourself Accountable

Track your progress and celebrate your wins, no matter how seemingly small or insignificant. It ALL counts. Self-accountability fosters a sense of accomplishment and encourages further growth.

By practicing discipline, you create a structured environment that supports your authenticity. You become more in tune with your needs and more capable of meeting them.

Being authentic isn't just a feel-good concept; it's a practical strategy for achieving balance and success in your professional and personal life. By showing up as your true self, setting boundaries, and mastering self-discipline, you lay the foundation for a life that aligns with your values and aspirations. Listen to my favorite affirmations by scanning the Balance Blueprint.

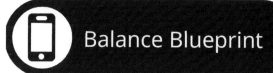

Balance Blueprint

The Best You

Often people mistake authenticity for just showing up as you are. That's not authenticity, that's complacency. A more effective way to think about authenticity is to think about it as giving the best version or as I like to call it, your favorite version of yourself.

Showing up as the favorite version of yourself is crucial because it fosters authenticity and boosts your effectiveness in all areas of life. When you align with your true self, you unlock a sense of inner peace and confidence that allows you to interact more genuinely with others. Authenticity not only enhances personal relationships but also improves professional performance, as you are more likely to pursue goals and tasks that resonate with your core values. However, the path to becoming this ideal version of yourself can be challenging, especially if you don't take the time to slow down and reflect on who you truly want to be.

Authenticity has a profound impact on various aspects of our lives, shaping our interactions, decisions, and overall well-being. When individuals embrace their genuine selves, they foster stronger connections with others, as authenticity breeds trust and openness. This promotes deeper relationships, where individuals feel valued and understood. Furthermore, an authentic approach to life enhances creativity and innovation, as it encourages individuals to express themselves freely and explore their unique perspectives without the fear of judgment. In a professional context, authenticity can lead to greater job satisfaction and engagement, as individuals align their work with their personal values and goals. Ultimately, living authentically not only contributes to personal happiness and fulfillment but also cultivates a richer and more empathetic community. So, take the time to reflect on your true self and embrace it with confidence, as it is the key to becoming the best version of yourself.

By regularly exploring these questions, you'll gain clarity and direction on your path to becoming your favorite version of yourself. Additionally, it may be helpful to seek guidance from a therapist or life coach who can provide additional support and tools for self-discovery. Remember that this is a journey, and it's okay to not have all the answers right away. Be patient and kind to yourself as you continue to grow and evolve into the best version of yourself. And always remember, being authentic and true to yourself is the most important aspect of being your favorite version of yourself - everything else will fall into place with time and effort. So keep striving towards authenticity, because that's when you can truly have it all.

Balance Blueprint

Here are some reflection questions to get you started:

What activities make me lose track of time and feel most alive?

When do I feel most at peace and aligned with my values?

What qualities do I admire in others, and how can I cultivate them within myself?

What fears or doubts hold me back from being my favorite version of myself?

How can I create daily habits that support my journey toward authenticity?

What are three behaviors my favorite self would do daily?

What old messages or self-talk move me further away from my favorite self?

Section Two

RELENTLESS REST

"Almost everything will work again if you unplug it for a little while, especially you"-Anne Lamont

Relentless Rest in Real Life

I pulled up to a local coffee shop eager to talk to Jared, a senior software developer. I was especially excited to hear a male's perspective on work-life balance. So, I just sat back and listened. Here's what Jared had to say about relentless rest:

"As a father, husband, and professional, my life is a whirlwind of responsibilities. For the longest time, I juggled everything without giving much thought to rest, and it started to take a toll on me. I learned that setting boundaries and knowing when to say no is key. It's not possible to do everything in one day; you have to prioritize.

In the beginning, prioritizing rest felt almost impossible. There was always something to be done, and guilt would creep in whenever I tried to take a break. But I realized that without proper rest, I wasn't able to give my best to my family or my work. I needed at least six hours of sleep to function well, so I planned my days around that, ensuring I didn't overcommit.

Growing up, rest was always about preparing for the next day, whether it was for school or church. It was more functional than restorative. As an adult, I struggled with feeling guilty about needing rest. There was always a fire to put out or something to fix, which made it hard to fully relax.

Over time, I came to understand that rest is crucial. Without it, I became irritable and resentful, and even the smallest issues seemed like big problems. I noticed a significant drop in my mental health and realized that without rest, I couldn't be the best version of myself for my wife and kids. I started to take shortcuts, which wasn't good for anyone.

What helped me most was setting a specific time to wind down and go to bed. This routine has become more effective now that my kids are older. I used to try and steal back time at the end of the day to relax, but that often backfired, stealing away my rest instead.

If I could talk to my younger self, I'd tell him to slow down, give himself grace, and understand that it's okay to make mistakes. Leading with love and learning from those mistakes is essential. I'd also emphasize the importance of not assigning artificial timelines based on others' expectations. Being an adult and a parent is hard work, but setting boundaries and prioritizing rest makes it a lot more manageable."

Jared's Approach to Work-Life Balance

Jared emphasizes the importance of setting clear boundaries between work and family life to achieve a healthy work-life balance. His experience with a demanding job early in his career taught him the necessity of prioritizing his personal time, leading him to refine his ability to say no to additional workload when necessary. By being hands-on with his children and ensuring he is present for family moments, Jared demonstrates that success, for him, is about fulfilling family needs while excelling in his career. His strategy of establishing limits not only prevents work from overwhelming his personal life but also enhances his overall happiness and productivity. Jared's insights serve as a reminder to prioritize our well-being and relationships, even in the face of demanding careers. In today's fast-paced society, it is essential to find a balance between work and personal life to maintain long-term success and happiness. Jared believes that while rest is vital for overall well-being, a continuous pursuit of downtime without balance can be counterproductive. He asserts that there is a fine line between taking necessary breaks to recharge and becoming overly complacent. As Jared shows us, setting boundaries and being present for family moments can ultimately lead to truly having it all.

Understanding Relentless Rest

When it comes to striving for success, one concept often overlooked is the need for rest. In the hustle and bustle and ripping and running of our busy lives, taking time to rest might seem like a luxury we can't afford. However, true success isn't sustainable without incorporating rest into our daily routines. This chapter explores the concept of "Relentless Rest" and how prioritizing and redefining rest can lead to optimal performance.

Let's start with understanding what "Relentless Rest" means. The term "relentless" often conjures images of unwavering perseverance and determination. But what if we applied that same energy to our need for rest? Relentless rest means making rest a non-negotiable priority, no matter the circumstances. It means not compromising on your need for rejuvenation and ensuring that rest is an integral non-negotiable part of your routine. Repeat after me, "I don't play about my rest" and feel free to add head or hand gestures while saying it.

Our mind, and early messages from our upbringing, often deceive us into thinking that resting will set us back or cause us to fall behind, (take a moment to think about all of the popular songs about work, money, hustle, and success); however, being relentless about rest requires an internal dialogue where you convince yourself of its importance. It's a mindset shift and an "inside job" that you'll need to master.

Rest is another vital aspect of maintaining balance and boundaries. In our hustle culture, rest is often seen as a luxury rather than a necessity. However, rest is crucial for your brain's health and overall productivity. Redefine rest as a mandatory and guilt-free part of your life and well-being and as the catalyst to productivity.

When clients come to me saying they're tired, my initial question is, "What kind of tired?" There are many facets to exhaustion, including:

Physical Tiredness: The most obvious form of tiredness, relates to bodily fatigue.

Mental Tiredness: Fatigue caused by prolonged cognitive activities.

Emotional Tiredness: The result of continuous emotional stress or turmoil.

Spiritual Tiredness: Feeling disconnected from one's purpose or values.

Social Tiredness: Exhaustion from excessive social interactions.

Sensory Tiredness: Overstimulation from various sensory inputs.

Creative Tiredness: A lack of inspiration or creative drive.

Most people experience a combination of these types of tiredness. Identifying which form of exhaustion you're experiencing is crucial. This insight enables you to address your specific needs and recharge effectively.

Dr. Saundra Dalton-Smith, author of Sacred Rest, is the originator of the types of rest concept. STOP here and take the *Relentless Rest Quiz* to determine what type of "tired" you actually are.

Relentless Rest Quiz

The Types of Rest

Identifying the type of rest you need helps you to tailor your wellness practices. Here are practical tips to address different types of tiredness:

Physical Rest: Engage in activities that promote bodily relaxation, such as gentle yoga, stretching, or taking a warm bath.

Mental Rest: Allocate time for mental breaks. Read a book, meditate, or practice mindfulness.

Emotional Rest: Seek emotional support from friends or a therapist. Journaling can also help process emotions.

Spiritual Rest: Spend time in nature, pray, or engage in activities that bring you a sense of purpose.

Social Rest: Take breaks from social media and set boundaries for social interactions.

Sensory Rest: Limit screen time, reduce noise levels, and create a calming environment.

Creative Rest: Allow yourself to be inspired by different forms of art or take a break from creating to regain your creativity.

The Science of Rest

Rest isn't laziness; it's a necessary component of high performance. Your brain needs downtime to process and rejuvenate. The glymphatic system, or what I like to call the street sweeping system, responsible for clearing waste from the brain, functions optimally during rest. Without sufficient rest, you can't operate at your best. This system removes toxins or "trash and clutter" that build up during the day. It plays a crucial role in maintaining brain health. During sleep, particularly during the deep sleep stages, this system becomes highly active, allowing cerebrospinal fluid to flow more freely throughout the brain. This process helps wash away harmful substances, including beta-amyloid—a protein associated with Alzheimer's disease—and other metabolic waste that accumulates during waking hours.

Prioritizing sleep means keeping this system running efficiently, which translates to better cognitive function and overall brain health.

To effectively activate the glymphatic system and ensure optimal brain function, adults typically require between 6 to 8 hours of quality sleep each night. This duration facilitates the necessary stages of deep sleep, particularly slow-wave sleep (SWS) when the brain's waste clearance processes are at their peak. Research indicates that insufficient sleep can hinder the performance of the glymphatic system, potentially leading to a buildup of toxins and negatively impacting cognitive abilities (working memory, recall, processing, etc.). Therefore, prioritizing consistent, restorative sleep is vital for maintaining not only mental clarity but also overall brain health. Ensuring you have a restorative sleep environment—free from distractions and conducive to relaxation—can enhance glymphatic clearance, supporting a sharper, more resilient mind. Therefore, making sleep a priority is essential for high performers aiming to sustain their cognitive abilities and achieve long-term success. (Reddy OC, 2020 Nov 17;10(11):868)

Life at the top isn't just about achieving victories at every turn; it's about maintaining the stamina to enjoy those victories. Without consistent and intentional rest, even the most driven professionals will hit a wall. Let's explore further on how you can adopt the art of Relentless Rest, ensuring you stay sharp and resilient no matter what.

The Difference Between Rest and Sleep

While both rest and sleep are crucial for our well-being, they serve different purposes and functions. Sleep is a restorative state characterized by specific stages, including REM and deep sleep, during which our bodies undergo essential processes like cellular repair, memory consolidation, and hormone regulation. It is a passive state that requires us to be in a state of unconsciousness for full benefits.

On the other hand, rest is an active state of relaxation and reprieve that doesn't necessarily require sleep. It can involve taking breaks during work, meditative practices, enjoying leisure activities, or simply allowing our minds to wander. Rest helps reduce stress, recharge mental energy, and enhance focus. While sleep is vital for physical restoration, rest fosters mental clarity and emotional stability, making both essential components of a balanced and productive life.

The Danger of Not Resting

As important as rest may be, many people still struggle to prioritize it. In a culture that values productivity and success above all else, taking time for rest can sometimes be seen as a weakness or laziness. However, the consequences of not resting can have serious long-term effects on our health and performance.

Chronic lack of rest can lead to burnout, which is a state of emotional, physical, and mental exhaustion caused by prolonged wakefulness.

Prioritize Sleep

Sleep is the ultimate form of rest, yet it's often the first thing we sacrifice. Quality sleep is non-negotiable for maintaining peak performance. A good night's sleep doesn't just recharge your body; it rejuvenates your mind, enhancing decision-making, creativity, and emotional resilience.

Ensuring Quality Sleep

Quality sleep is non-negotiable. Aim for six to eight hours of sleep each night. While some people claim to function on less, optimal performance requires adequate rest. There are so many devices that can help track your sleep and ensure you're getting the rest you need (if you follow me, you already know my favorite sleep tracker ring).

At the end of each day, tell yourself that you've done enough, that you are enough, and that it's time to rest. This self-affirmation reassures your mind and body that it's okay to wind down and recharge.

Remember, even professionals like myself struggle with these practices. I am a reformed night owl and some of my friends and even colleagues STILL send me 2am messages because they are accustomed to the "old me". So listen, it's okay to face challenges because perfection is not the goal. The beauty is in your ability to course correct and bounce back.

Establish a Nighttime Routine

Remember when you were a kid and nap time and bedtime was a huge deal? A bedtime routine isn't just for kids. Establishing a consistent nighttime routine signals to your body that it's time to wind down. This could include activities like reading a book, taking a warm bath, or practicing mindfulness exercises. Does bath time and a book sound familiar? History tends to repeat itself. The key is consistency—performing the same actions every night can significantly improve your sleep quality.

Tips to Establish a Nighttime Routine
Creating an effective nighttime routine can greatly enhance the quality of your sleep and prepare your mind and body for rest. It doesn't have to be complicated. When in doubt, think about what young kids need for a good night's sleep. Here are some practical tips to help you establish a nighttime routine that promotes relaxation and signals it's time for bed:

Set a Consistent Sleep Schedule: Aim to go to bed and wake up at the same time every day, even on weekends. This consistency helps regulate your body's internal clock and improves sleep quality over time. It even helps to go outside first thing in the morning so that your circadian rhythm can be naturally activated.

Limit Screen Time: Reduce exposure to screens (TV, phones, tablets) at least an hour before bedtime. The blue light emitted from devices can interfere with melatonin production, making it harder to fall asleep. Blue light glasses and smart phone light settings help some, but it's not worth the risk.

Create a Relaxing Environment: Make your sleeping space comfortable and conducive to rest. Dim the lights, reduce noise, and ensure a cool room temperature to promote relaxation. I use a sleep mask, ear plugs, a weighted blanket, and black out curtains. I laugh at myself every time I think about all of the pageantry around bed time.

Incorporate Mindfulness Practices: Consider adding activities such as meditation, deep breathing exercises, or gentle stretching to your routine. These practices can help calm your mind and prepare your body for sleep. There are countless apps and You Tube videos for sleep meditation.

Wind Down with a Good Book: Reading a physical book can be a great way to unwind. Choose something enjoyable but not overly stimulating to help ease your transition into sleep.

Limit Caffeine and Heavy Meals: Avoid consuming caffeine and heavy meals close to bedtime. Instead, opt for light snacks if you're hungry and herbal teas to promote relaxation. Digestion requires a significant amount of energy and can keep your body awake. Get rid of the night cap as well. Alcohol is notorious for sleep disturbance.

Establish a Pre-Sleep Ritual: Develop a series of calming activities that you perform each night. This could include journaling, practicing gratitude, or taking a warm bath—whatever helps you to unwind and signal to your body that it's time for rest. Pro-tip— give your brain explicit permission to rest. I say something like this to myself every night "RJ you did pretty good today girl. You can rest. You're done. Get some rest and start fresh tomorrow."

By incorporating these tips into your evening routine, you'll be better prepared to embrace restful sleep, ultimately supporting your cognitive function and overall well-being.

Finding Balance

The key to adopting Relentless Rest is finding a balance between work and rest. It's not about giving up on your goals or slowing down, but rather understanding that rest is an integral part of achieving success.

One way to find balance is by incorporating rest into your daily routine. This can be as simple as taking short breaks throughout the day or scheduling dedicated downtime after a busy period.

Another important aspect of finding balance is setting boundaries. Learn to say no when you feel overwhelmed and prioritize self-care. Remember, you cannot pour from an empty cup. Get used to me repeating this.

Putting It into Practice

Now that we understand the importance of rest and finding balance, let's summarize practical ways to incorporate Relentless Rest into our lives:

Start your day with a morning routine that includes time for reflection, relaxation, or exercise. A morning routine is just as important as a night routine.

Take breaks throughout the day to recharge and refocus. This could be a short walk outside or even just closing your eyes for a few minutes.

Schedule regular days off in addition to vacations to completely disconnect from work and recharge. I schedule a quarterly vacation in addition to a family vacation and a couple's vacation. You can work your way up to it, but I know way too many executives who never use their PTO or vacation days even if they don't roll over. Start small with 3-4 day staycations. The key is to pencil them in on your schedule in advance.

Prioritize sleep by setting a consistent bedtime and creating a relaxing sleep environment.

Find activities that bring you joy and make time for them regularly. This could be anything from reading, painting, cooking, or spending time with loved ones. A great strategy is to schedule the activities you love.

Remember that rest looks different for everyone. It's important to find what works best for you and prioritize it in your daily life. The rested version of you will run circles around the exhausted version any day. Productivity and effectiveness are exponentially greater when rest is regularly and intentionally incorporated.

Predefine Done

Ever notice how work never really "ends"? There's always another email to answer, another project to complete, and another meeting to attend. This is where the concept of "Predefine Done" comes into play. Predefining what "done" looks like for your day means setting specific, achievable goals and knowing when to clock out. It's about permitting yourself to rest, knowing that you've completed what you set out to do. This helps prevent the feeling of never-ending work and allows you to fully disconnect and recharge during your downtime.

Furthering the Concept of Predefine Done
To effectively implement the concept of "Predefine Done," it's essential to establish clear boundaries for both your work and personal life. Begin by outlining your daily goals and breaking them down into manageable tasks. Prioritize these tasks based on urgency and importance, allowing yourself to focus on what truly matters. In other words, what MUST be done?

At the end of each day, take a moment to assess your progress. Ask yourself: What did I achieve today? Was it enough to consider the day a success? If so, how do I know? What are the success metrics or KPIs? By celebrating your accomplishments, no matter how small, you reinforce the concept that you've reached a satisfactory point of completion.

Additionally, consider using tools such as to-do lists or digital task management apps to visually track what you've completed. This creates a tangible representation of your achievements and helps you recognize when you've reached your limit. I still use an old school pad and paper at my desk along with my favorite hotel pen. Some of my clients use super sophisticated calendars and apps. Find what works for you and be consistent.

Finally, don't hesitate to communicate your boundaries to colleagues and supervisors, ensuring they understand when you are "done" for the day. This fosters an environment where taking breaks and prioritizing rest is respected and valued. By mastering this skill, you empower yourself to disconnect from work, engage fully in your personal life, and prevent burnout.

Focus on What MUST Be Done

Not everything on your to-do list carries the same weight. The trick is to focus on what must be done rather than what could be done. There's always something that could be done. Prioritize tasks that will have the most significant impact and align with your long-term goals. This approach ensures that your energy is spent wisely and allows more room for rest. Remember, quality over quantity. We'll talk more about how to focus on what must be done, in the next section.

How to Focus on What MUST Be Done

Focusing on what must be done involves honing in on tasks that have the greatest impact on your goals and well-being. Start by employing the 80/20 rule, also known as the Pareto Principle, which suggests that 80% of your results come from 20% of your efforts. Identify those critical tasks that contribute significantly to your success and prioritize them over less important activities.

To achieve this, create a priority matrix by categorizing your tasks based on urgency and importance. Tasks that are both urgent and important should take precedence; these are the activities that demand your immediate attention. For tasks that are important but not urgent, set deadlines to ensure they are completed on time without becoming last-minute crises. Meanwhile, tasks that are neither urgent nor important can often be delegated or eliminated entirely, freeing up your time for more meaningful work.

Scan the QR code and download a free template of a priority matrix to divide your tasks in a meaningful way.

Balance Blueprint

Regularly reviewing and adjusting your priorities is also crucial. At the beginning of each week, take a moment to reflect on your goals and upcoming projects, allowing yourself to reset your focus. By doing this, you create a roadmap that directs your attention to what truly matters, enabling you to allocate your energy efficiently and make room for the rejuvenating rest that is essential for sustained productivity. I find that regular review is what allows me to stay ahead of my to-do list tasks.

To Don't List

Yes, you read that right—a "To Don't" list! Just as important as knowing what to do is knowing what not to do. Identify activities and habits that drain your energy with little to no return. By actively eliminating these, you're clearing mental clutter and making more space for restorative downtime.

Creating a "To Don't" List

Creating a "To Don't" list is an effective strategy for managing your time and energy more efficiently. Start by reflecting on your daily activities and identifying those tasks or habits that no longer serve your goals or well-being. These may include time-consuming meetings that lack purpose, social obligations that feel draining, or unproductive distractions, such as excessive social media use.

Once you've pinpointed these activities, write them down in a dedicated space, ensuring that your list is visible and accessible. This serves as a constant reminder of what to avoid in order to maintain clarity and focus. Next, consider implementing actionable steps to limit these activities. For instance, if you find that certain meetings are consistently unproductive, establish clear criteria for attending them or suggest alternative communication methods. Similarly, if distractions like social media consume excessive time, set specific time limits for their use or designate them as "no-go" zones during productive hours.

Regularly review and update your "To Don't" list as your circumstances and priorities change. This dynamic approach will help you stay committed to avoiding tasks that drain your energy and prevent you from fully embracing the restorative practices that lead to a balanced life. By actively managing what you choose to negate, you cultivate a more focused, fulfilling daily experience. Say it with me, "What I'm NOT going to do is..." Or you can simply visualize the tasks you will stop doing so that you will no longer be tyrannized by tiny tasks.

Download your "to-don't list" right away. You can add to it gradually.

Balance Blueprint

Say No, Again

The power of saying "No" cannot be overstated. For high-performing professionals, the demand for your time and attention can be overwhelming. It's crucial to understand that saying "No" to one thing often means saying "Yes" to more meaningful opportunities—and more importantly, to rest. If it doesn't align with your priorities or add value, feel empowered to decline.

Saying No to Family and Friends

It can be particularly challenging to say "No" to family and friends, as these are the people we care about deeply and wish to support and they think that they are the exception to the rule. For example, when I put my phone on do not disturb, my son presses the "notify anyway" option. Has this happened to you?

Setting boundaries with loved ones is just as essential as it is with colleagues. Begin by understanding that prioritizing your well-being does not diminish your love or commitment to them. When faced with requests from family or friends, take a moment to assess whether fulfilling these requests aligns with your current capacity and priorities. Is it something you really want to do? Or as my business consultant Marquel Russell asks me, "Is it a HECK YEA? Does it get you closer to your goals?" If not, practice saying no.

To communicate your decision effectively, express your feelings honestly while maintaining empathy. You might say something like, "I really appreciate you considering me for this, but I wouldn't be able to give the 100 percent you deserve" This approach validates their request while asserting your need for space. Remember, maintaining your health and rest ultimately benefits your relationships, as it allows you to be more present and engaged when you do spend time with those you care about.

Why Do High Performers Have a Hard Time Saying No?

High performers often struggle with the concept of saying "No" due to a combination of intrinsic and extrinsic pressures, and possibly even a people-pleasing problem. Internally, their drive for success and achievement can lead to an ingrained belief that they must be constantly available and responsive to every request. This relentless pursuit of excellence may foster a fear of letting others down or missing out on opportunities, which can translate into an overwhelming sense of obligation to agree to tasks and projects, regardless of their alignment with personal goals. In Executive Burnout, I reference how being a first generation college graduate is associated with a number of stressors, one of which is being the sole supporter to the family of origin while learning to navigate the executive landscape for yourself.

Societal expectations and workplace cultures that glorify busyness further complicate this issue when in reality, many are busy doing nothing. High achievers may feel that their worth is directly tied to their productivity, leading them to overcommit themselves to maintain an image of reliability and diligence. They become the "rockstar" who never gets the promotion because they've branded themselves as doers and not innovators. I'm talking about them though, not you.

The cumulative effect of these pressures can create a cycle in which saying "No" feels not only daunting but also counterproductive, making it crucial for high performers to actively cultivate the skill of setting boundaries in order to protect their time and energy for what truly matters.

Have you ever felt like you were too busy to get your own work done either in your personal or professional life? Here's a tip, keep on saying no with confidence and intention, and remember that it's not about avoiding tasks altogether but rather prioritizing what truly matters to you so that you can show up as the best version of you (not the exhausted resentful version). With these skills in hand, you can achieve success without sacrificing your well-being or relationships along the way.

Have you ever asked someone to do something, and they said yes, but then either complained the whole time or did a mediocre job? That is exactly why saying no is good for both sides. Saying no gives you more energy for your "yes". Imagine that every time you show up, people automatically know it's going to be amazing because you aren't spread too thin.

In the relentless pursuit of success and balance, rest is your secret weapon. By implementing strategies like Predefining Done, focusing on essential tasks, creating a "To Don't" list, saying no, prioritizing sleep, and establishing a nighttime routine, you can achieve a state of Restful Resilience. Remember, relentless rest isn't about being lazy; it's about being smart with your energy so that you can show up as your best self, day after day. So go ahead, prioritize rest, and watch your decision-making abilities, creativity, and emotional resilience soar to new heights. Your future self will thank you for it.

Keep striving for your version of success with a well-rested mind and body.

Access a balanced lifestyle with the A.R.T. of Balance course, specifically designed for busy professionals seeking practical and holistic strategies to integrate balance into their daily routines. This course is an investment in your overall well-being, helping you to find harmony and fulfillment in both your personal and professional life.

Scan the QR code if you're ready to take your work-life balance to the next level.

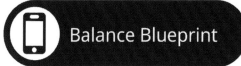

Section Three

TIME CONSCIOUSNESS

"The bad news is that time flies. The good news is that YOU are the pilot." - Michael Altshuler

I n the final section, we will explore the third step of the A.R.T of Balance– Time Consciousness. This is all about managing our time effectively to achieve a balanced life. We'll discuss the concept of time consciousness and how it can help us shift from feeling overwhelmed by time to feeling in control of it. We'll also provide practical techniques for effective time management and maintaining a balance between work and personal time called 'key points'. They are designed to provide a convenient and easy way to immediately implement the ideas. But first, let's explore my time with Dr. Will.

I settled into my home office, ready for another eye-opening conversation. This time, I was meeting with Dr. Will, a successful online coach whose entrepreneurial spirit had led him down a variety of interesting paths. The video call began with the usual pleasantries and I invited Dr. Will to relax and be himself.

"Okay," I began, adjusting my microphone. "This will just be a regular conversation. Just be yourself and tell me your story."

Dr. Will leaned back, the story of his career spilling out effortlessly. "For work? So what I do now is I'm an online coach. I was a school teacher for eight years teaching special education, up until the pandemic. And right near the end of it, I got into the online space, meaning making money from home. I got into government contracting first, did that for a year or two, and made good money doing that. Then I moved into the coaching space alongside what I do now. Now it's a combination of working from home and dealing with that new, you know, type of life of working from home, you know, twenty-four seven."

I paused at the "twenty-four seven" and jotted down some notes for later. "Would you consider yourself a CEO, entrepreneur, or anything like that?"

Dr. Will's face lit up with pride. "Hundred percent. I definitely write the word CEO on the documents that I submit to the government. I'm also an entrepreneur because I'm always thinking of new businesses and how to expand current ones. Hundred percent."

I chuckled, sensing Dr. Will's passion. "Right. What other roles do you play outside of being a CEO and an entrepreneur?"

Dr. Will softened a bit, his mind shifting to his personal life. "Well, outside of work, I'm a husband, a dog dad, a son, brother, and uncle to six nieces and nephews. So, yeah, a lot of roles."

"And how significant are you to all of those people?" I asked, genuinely curious.

"I feel that I'm very significant to all those people. I feel like I'm the center for all those people," Dr. Will responded with a hint of responsibility in his voice.

I nodded, understanding the weight of such a role. "Okay. So you're the center for your business, and you're the center for your family and extended family."

"Correct. Mhmm," Dr. Will agreed.

I leaned in, becoming more serious. "What are some challenges you've had with that?"

"The biggest challenge, I would say, is time management. You start to realize that so many things are pulling you in one direction. My mother, for instance—she just retired this year. It's great for her, but it's also like, 'Hey. I'm at home. I'm free.

What's up?' There's the desire to spend time with loved ones, but then there's also the time you need to spend on your business as an entrepreneur and CEO. Balancing or prioritizing time is the biggest thing I've had to do since leaving teaching."

I listened intently, absorbing every word. "How so?"

"Well, now work is home. You gotta work harder at the boundaries because work is home. This office that I'm in now is work. Walking out means I'm no longer at work, but with technology—your phone, Slack channels—the good thing is we're connected, but the bad thing is we're connected. It's hard to unplug sometimes."

"And so what are some of the downfalls of having a difficult time unplugging?" I asked and allowed the silence to fill the virtual space.

Dr. Will sighed, feeling the weight of the question. "The downfalls? It's just... you end up going nonstop. You'd go to the point of burnout if you didn't put things in place. Before implementing boundaries and unplugging, it was very burnout-ish. Pulled from family, pulled from business, not knowing how to set boundaries. Some days, I didn't want to do anything."

I nodded, kept writing, and then asked. "What was your life like before you started setting boundaries and unplugging specifically for you?"

"Close to burnout. I mean, that's debatable for each person, but for me, it was being pulled from all angles. I read a book called 'Buy Back Your Time,' and it talked about business owners who sabotage their business because they just don't want to deal with everything. I was close to that until I got these resources."

"How is your business doing now as it relates to revenue?" I asked, shifting gears.

"Business has gone great. Revenue is trending up. We're on pace to hit our goals for the year. The last few months have been quarter-million-dollar months, and one month even hit three hundred thousand. It's come a long way since I started in 2022 with 38K months."

"So what I'm hearing is that because of issues with time management and setting boundaries, you almost subconsciously blew up or closed a multimillion-dollar business. Is that accurate?" I clarified.

"That's accurate," Dr. Will admitted.

I leaned forward, eager to hear more. "Tell me some of the techniques that work for you as it relates to time management or being conscious of time."

"Like I said before, the biggest thing is getting a calendar and sticking to it. One of my pastors once said, 'If you have a budget but don't follow it, then you don't have a budget.' It's the same for a calendar. Having a system to manage your time is crucial."

The conversation continued, rich with insights and experiences. It was clear that Dr. Will had come a long way from his days as a school teacher, navigating the complexities of entrepreneurship with resilience and a newfound sense of balance.

As Dr. Will's story shows, with the right strategies and mindset, it's possible to find harmony between work and life, even in the most challenging times. It's a constant journey, but one that ultimately leads to personal and professional success, just as it did for Dr. Will.

In today's digital age, it's easy to get lost in the constant buzz of notifications and emails from our cell phones. We often find ourselves chained to our devices, unable to disconnect even for a moment without slight panic. This constant connectedness can have detrimental effects on our mental health, productivity, and overall well-being.

Do you think I'm exaggerating? Put your phone and any other communication devices (yes your smart watch too) in another room for the next 30 minutes while you're reading this book. Pay attention to your thoughts and feelings.

The Illusion of Multitasking

One of the most pervasive myths of the digital age is the idea that multitasking makes us more efficient. The reality, however, is quite different. When we switch between tasks, our brains require time to adjust and refocus, resulting in cognitive "switch costs." Studies have shown that frequent task-switching can reduce productivity by up to 40%. Instead of completing tasks more quickly, we end up doing them less efficiently and with a greater likelihood of errors. It takes me about 20 minutes per interruption to get back on track. Research indicates that I'm not alone.

Modern technology has made it possible to be reachable at all times, but this constant connectivity comes at a price. Notifications from emails, social media, and messaging apps create an environment of perpetual distraction. Each interruption, no matter how brief, disrupts our flow and concentration, making it difficult to achieve deep, focused work.

Key Points:

The Cognitive Load: The human brain is not designed to handle multiple complex tasks simultaneously. Constant notifications and digital interruptions increase cognitive load, leading to mental fatigue and overall exhaustion causing you to ask yourself, "Why am I always so tired?"

Increased Error Rates: Multitasking can lead to higher error rates. Errors can be costly in terms of both time and resources, further reducing overall productivity.

Reduced Quality of Work: The quality of our work suffers when we frequently switch tasks, as we are less likely to engage deeply and thoughtfully with any single task.

The Attention Economy: Many digital platforms are designed to capture and hold our attention. Social media apps, for instance, use algorithms to keep us engaged, often at the expense of our productivity.

Interrupted Workflow: Interruptions are costly. Research indicates that it takes an average of 23 minutes to regain focus after an interruption. With frequent disruptions, significant portions of the workday are lost to regaining concentration.

Mental Fatigue: Continuous exposure to notifications and digital stimuli can lead to mental fatigue, reducing our ability to stay focused and productive over time.

The Myth of Availability

There is a growing expectation in the modern workplace that employees must be constantly available and responsive. This expectation can lead to a culture of "presenteeism," where employees feel pressured to be online and accessible, even during off-hours. This perpetual state of availability can be detrimental to both productivity and well-being. This also happens in our personal lives with the expectation of immediate response no matter what the request is.

Key Points:

Work-Life Balance: The blurred lines between work and personal life can lead to burnout. Professionals who are always "on" are less likely to take the necessary breaks to recharge, ultimately reducing their productivity. I describe it as being "busy doing nothing".

Stress and Anxiety: The pressure to respond promptly to messages and emails can create stress and anxiety, further impairing productivity and job satisfaction.

Reduced Innovation: Constant connectivity leaves little room for downtime, which is essential for creativity and innovative thinking. Without breaks, leaders are less likely to come up with new ideas and solutions.

Information Overload

In the digital age, we have access to more information than ever before. While this abundance of information can be valuable, it can also be overwhelming. The constant influx of data, emails, and updates can lead to information overload, making it difficult to discern what is truly important and relevant.

Key Points:

Decision Fatigue: The need to constantly sift through vast amounts of information can lead to decision fatigue. When our cognitive resources are depleted, we are more likely to make poor decisions or procrastinate.

Reduced Focus: Information overload can scatter our focus, making it challenging to concentrate on a single task or project. This scattered attention can hinder our ability to complete tasks efficiently.

Decreased Retention: When bombarded with excessive information, our ability to retain and recall important details diminishes. This can lead to mistakes and a lack of continuity in our work.

The Need for Digital Detox

To counteract the negative impact of constant connectivity, many experts advocate for regular digital detoxes. By setting boundaries and creating designated "tech-free" times, busy professionals can reclaim their focus and productivity.

Key Points:

Scheduled Breaks: Implementing scheduled breaks from technology can help restore mental clarity and reduce stress. Techniques such as the Pomodoro Technique which was described earlier can be effective in balancing focused work and rest periods.

Mindfulness Practices: Incorporating mindfulness practices, such as meditation and deep breathing exercises, can help individuals manage stress and improve concentration.

Creating Boundaries: Establishing clear boundaries for technology use, such as turning off notifications during work hours or setting specific times for checking emails, can help maintain focus and productivity.

Visit the Balance Blueprint for mindfulness meditation exercises you can use to enhance your time-consciousness.

Time Consciousness In Real Life

Dr. Evans's office was a hub of organized chaos. Papers were neatly stacked, yet the constant buzz of activity and the chatter of students and staff outside the door indicated a day in full swing. This was the workspace of a man who thrived on structure amidst the whirlwind of a high school environment.

I sat across from Dr. Evans, ready to capture the essence of a conversation that would later be transcribed into something more vivid than mere words on paper. My goal was to uncover the real voice of executives like Dr. Evans—those actively striving to find balance in their demanding roles.

"Tell me a little bit about yourself and what your day-to-day life is like during the school year," I prompted, even though after being in the school for about thirty minutes, I felt like I already knew.

Dr. Evans, still getting comfortable with the idea of sharing his day-to-day organized chaos, began hesitantly, "Oh, wow. During the school year? A little bit about myself and what my day-to-day life is like during the school year." He paused, considering how to encapsulate his experiences. "Yes. If I start babbling on too much, just let me know."

"No, the more, the better," I encouraged. "Take your time."

Dr. Evans chuckled before continuing, "I thought I would define myself as a first-generation college kid, but since my mom has an associate's degree, I guess I fall out of that category. Still, I was definitely the first to get any kind of advanced degree. I ended up at Morris Brown, thinking I'd teach math, only to discover they didn't offer that major. I majored in math anyway and, yada yada yada, got a PhD in math—even though I didn't take any advanced math classes."

He laughed, reminiscing about the winding path that led him to his current role. "Over the years, I transitioned from teaching math to holding various administrative roles, and finally, I was promoted to principal. My days as an assistant principal felt more controlled. Now, everyone else seems to control my day."

I nodded, understanding the shift in dynamics. "Do you feel like with this fast-paced role that it's possible to have a work-life balance?"

"It is," Dr. Evans affirmed, "but it requires a lot of learning and discipline. I preach it a lot, you know. That's actually how you and I met. I was struggling with balance in my new role and looking for help. Your strategies were so impactful that I shared them with the leadership team. It was infectious—it spread through the building, improving our culture dramatically."

He pulled out a piece of paper, reading from his notes. "Our culture survey showed we had one of the highest satisfaction rates in the cluster—over seventy percent, a twelve percent increase from the previous year."

"Wow," I exclaimed. "That's impressive. And it sounds like culture was always a top priority for you." I was quietly amused to find out that my course on balance and burnout (which you can find at bonus. artofbalancebook.com) made such an impact on the school in a short time.

"Absolutely," Dr. Evans agreed. "But achieving balance has to start from the top, and I'll admit I don't always practice what I preach. There was a time after winter break when my foot was killing me. One of the assistant principals finally called me out for not taking care of myself. They sent me home, telling me not to come back until I was better. It made me feel proud that they cared enough to hold me accountable."

I smiled, sensing a pivotal moment. "If you had to choose one of the three pillars of balance—authenticity, relentless rest, and time consciousness—which one resonates most with you right now?"

"Time consciousness," Dr. Evans responded without hesitation. "Being more efficient with my time is crucial. If I'm not careful, meetings drag on, and I end up doing tasks that could be delegated. I've started using the priority matrix to help with this."

"That's perfect," I said, my excitement evident. "I'm dedicating an entire section of my book to these types of techniques. What are some strategies that have worked for you in managing your time?"

"My calendar," Dr. Evans answered. "If it's not on my calendar, it doesn't exist. I try to give people their time, but they need to respect my schedule too. Living by my calendar has made a world of difference. If I weren't disciplined about it, I'd be blown around by everyone else's priorities and never get my own work done."

I leaned in, capturing every word. I've had thousands of successful clients over a span of almost two decades, and I still get excited by every single win that my clients experience. The conversation had transformed into a powerful narrative about time consciousness—a real-life account that would resonate with executives, entrepreneurs, and professionals striving for balance.

Our discussion reflected the essence of the book's title—The A.R.T. of Balance™. It wasn't just about surviving the daily grind but mastering the art of balancing authenticity, relentless rest, and time consciousness to lead a fulfilling and effective life.

Practical Strategies for Time Consciousness

Time consciousness can be developed through various practical strategies that individuals can incorporate into their daily lives. Some effective techniques include:

Creating a schedule: As Dr. Evans mentioned, having a calendar and scheduling tasks can be an effective way to manage time. It allows individuals to plan their day and allocate time for specific tasks, ensuring that important responsibilities are not overlooked.

Prioritizing tasks: A priority matrix, as mentioned in the conversation, is a useful tool for prioritizing tasks based on urgency and importance. This helps individuals focus on high-priority tasks first and avoid getting overwhelmed with less critical responsibilities.

Delegating responsibilities: Learning to delegate tasks to others can help individuals free up valuable time for more important priorities. Delegation also promotes teamwork and allows individuals to focus on their strengths and areas of expertise.

Avoiding distractions: In today's digital age, it's easy to get distracted by social media and other forms of technology. Setting boundaries and minimizing distractions can help individuals stay focused on their tasks and manage time more effectively.

Taking breaks: It may seem counterintuitive, but taking regular breaks can actually improve productivity and time consciousness. Short breaks throughout the day allow individuals to recharge and refocus, leading to better time management in the long run.

So, what are the tangible benefits of maintaining a calendar for a busy executive like yourself? I like to refer to my calendar as my board of directors. No decisions are made without consulting my BOD.

First and foremost, a calendar provides clarity and focus. By having a clear visual representation of your commitments, you can easily identify what needs your attention and when. This helps in minimizing the risk of overcommitting and ensures that you are allocating time to high-priority tasks.

Secondly, it enhances productivity. With a well-structured calendar, you can set realistic deadlines and break down larger projects into manageable tasks. This allows you to maintain a steady workflow and avoid last-minute stress.

Another significant advantage is improved time management. Executives often juggle multiple responsibilities; a calendar helps in scheduling time slots for each activity, reducing the likelihood of conflicting events. This way, you're better positioned to meet both professional and personal obligations without compromising on either.

Additionally, a calendar can serve as a tool for strategic planning. By mapping out your long-term goals and tracking ongoing projects, you can better align your daily activities with your broader objectives. This ensures that your daily efforts are contributing to your long-term success.

Lastly, maintaining a calendar promotes work-life balance. A glance at your calendar can help you ensure that you are also allocating time for self-care, family, and leisure activities, which are crucial for overall well-being.

In summary, maintaining a calendar is not just about keeping track of appointments and deadlines; it's about structuring your time in a way that facilitates better decision-making and a more balanced, productive life.

Here are some tips to ensure your calendar remains an effective tool:

Regularly Update: Dedicate a few minutes each day to review and update your calendar.

Color Coding: Use different colors for different types of tasks (e.g., red for urgent meetings, blue for personal time).

Set Reminders: Leverage reminder features to notify you ahead of important events.

Review Weekly: At the beginning of each week, take a moment to plan and review your upcoming schedule.

The Priority Matrix, as briefly mentioned earlier, also known as the Eisenhower Box, is a powerful tool to help you decide on and prioritize tasks by urgency and importance. It divides tasks into four quadrants:

Urgent and Important (Do): Tasks you should do immediately.

Not Urgent but Important (Delay): Tasks you should schedule to do later.

Urgent but Not Important (Delegate): Tasks you should delegate if possible.

Not Urgent and Not Important (Delete): Tasks you should eliminate.

For busy executives, the Priority Matrix is an invaluable tool because it provides a structured approach to time management and decision-making. Here's why it is essential:

The Priority Matrix enhances focus and clarity. By categorizing tasks based on their urgency and importance, executives can easily identify which tasks demand immediate attention and which can be scheduled or delegated. This prevents the mental clutter of trying to juggle multiple priorities simultaneously.

It improves productivity and efficiency. By focusing on tasks that are both urgent and important, executives can ensure that their energy and resources are being directed towards activities that have the highest impact on their goals. This streamlining of efforts helps in achieving more in less time.

It reduces stress and overwhelm. The Priority Matrix makes it easier to see which tasks can be deferred or eliminated, thus preventing the common pitfall of trying to do everything at once.

This methodical approach helps in maintaining a manageable workload.

Moreover, the Priority Matrix aids in effective delegation. By identifying tasks that are urgent but not necessarily important, executives can delegate these tasks to their team members, freeing up their own time for more critical activities. This not only leverages the strengths of their team but also fosters a collaborative work environment.

Finally, it promotes strategic planning and long-term success. The matrix encourages executives to dedicate time to important but not urgent tasks, such as strategic planning and personal development, which are often overlooked in the daily hustle but are crucial for long-term growth and success.

In summary, the Priority Matrix equips busy executives with a practical framework to prioritize their tasks, ultimately leading to better time management, increased productivity, and a more balanced professional life.

To incorporate the Priority Matrix into your routine:

Daily Review: Spend 5-10 minutes each morning categorizing tasks into the matrix.

Focus Time: Allocate specific times of the day to focus on "Do" tasks – these are the ones that contribute to long-term success.

Delegate: Identify tasks in Quadrant 3 that can be delegated to others.

Eliminate: Be ruthless with Quadrant 4 tasks; they are distractions.

The Importance of Balance

The conversation between me and Dr. Evans also highlighted the underlying importance of balance in all aspects of life. It's not just about managing time effectively, but also finding a balance between work and personal life, prioritizing self-care, and being authentic to oneself.

In today's society, where success is often equated with constantly being busy and hustling, it's essential to recognize the value of balance. Neglecting one aspect of life in pursuit of another can lead to burnout, decreased productivity, and overall dissatisfaction.

As individuals strive for balance in their lives, they must also recognize that it's a continuous process. Priorities and responsibilities may shift over time, requiring adjustments in how time is managed and balance is achieved. It's about being intentional and staying true to one's values and priorities while adapting to changing circumstances.

Time consciousness plays a crucial role in achieving overall work-life balance. By mastering this aspect of life, individuals can take control of their schedule, prioritize tasks effectively, and find the right balance between work and personal life. Dr. Evans's story serves as a reminder that with dedication and the right strategies, anyone can achieve a fulfilling and successful life. The A.R.T. of Balance is a continuous journey, but one that can lead to a more authentic, restful, and time-conscious life.

Now let's talk about a touchy subject. I'm not scared of a little healthy confrontation, so here it goes.

But before we dive into the ways to break free from our cell phones, let's take a look at some of the negative effects of overusing them.

1. Mental Health Issues:

Constantly being connected to our cell phones can lead to heightened levels of stress and anxiety. The constant need to check for notifications and respond to messages can create a sense of urgency and pressure that can be overwhelming. This can also lead to feelings of FOMO (fear of missing out) and comparison, which can negatively impact our self-esteem and mental well-being. This happens with adults as much as it does with teens.

2. Decreased Productivity:

When we're constantly checking our phones, it's easy to get distracted and lose track of time. This can lead to decreased productivity and poor time management skills. The constant interruptions from our phones can also make it difficult to focus on important tasks, resulting in a decrease in quality work.

3. Disrupted Sleep Patterns:

The blue light emitted by cell phone screens can interfere with the body's natural production of melatonin, the hormone that helps us sleep. This can lead to difficulty falling asleep and disrupted sleep patterns, which can harm our overall health and well-being.

Ways to Break Free:

1. Set Boundaries for Phone Usage:

To break free from your cell phone, it's important to set boundaries for its usage. This could mean designating specific times of the day for checking emails and messages or setting a limit on social media scrolling time. It's also helpful to turn off notifications for non-urgent apps and only allow important ones to come through. I am a firm believer in using the "focus feature" or "do not disturb" to protect my time, even with my family.

2. Find Alternative Activities:

Instead of constantly reaching for your phone during downtime, find alternative activities that can help you disconnect. This could be anything from reading a book, going for a walk, or practicing meditation or mindfulness. These activities can provide a much-needed break from the constant stimulation of our phones and allow us to recharge. I know I'm not the only one who mindlessly picks up the phone and scrolls just out of habit. We'll have to help each other with this one.

3. Create No-Phone Zones:

Designating certain areas in your home or workplace as "no-phone zones" can help you disconnect and focus on the present moment without distractions. This could be your bedroom, dining table, or designated workspaces where phones are not allowed. For families, a mutual charging station is a great technique.

4. Use Tools to Limit Usage:

There are various apps and tools available that can help limit phone usage by setting time restrictions or blocking certain apps during designated times. These tools can act as a helpful reminder to disconnect and focus on other activities. I have to admit, when I get a reminder that I've been on Instagram too long, I feel a hint of rebellion for about 30 seconds.

5. Practice Mindful Phone Usage:

Finally, it's important to practice mindful phone usage. This means being aware of why you are reaching for your phone and setting intentions for its usage. Ask yourself if the activity is necessary or if it's simply a habit. Practicing mindfulness can help break the automatic response of constantly checking our phones and allow us to be more intentional with our time.

The Importance of Intentional Time Management

Remember Tangie, the C-Suite powerhouse? A game-changer for Tangie was enrolling in an executive burnout course. This experience equipped her with essential tools like intentional time management and calendar blocking. By being deliberate about her time, she's able to prioritize tasks and communicate her availability effectively.

Key Strategies Tangie Utilizes:

Time Blocking: Allocating specific times for work, family, and personal activities.

Over-Communicating: Being overly communicative about her schedule with team members and family members so that others can adjust their expectations accordingly.

Effective Communication with Family and Loved Ones

Tangie emphasizes the importance of clear and proactive communication with family and loved ones. She makes it a point to inform them when she'll be particularly busy, thus managing their expectations and reducing the feeling of being pulled in multiple directions. For instance, her family knows that January through March is her busiest period, and they adjust their demands on her time accordingly.

Recognizing and Communicating Personal Busy Periods

Being aware of her peak busy seasons and communicating them has provided Tangie with the space to focus on her work without feeling overwhelmed. This level of transparency allows her to accommodate essential tasks and also helps her family and colleagues to understand her constraints.

Learning and Applying New Tools

Tangie's approach to balance involves continuous learning and the application of new tools. She acknowledges that she's not inherently great at anything but has become proficient through hard work and the acquisition of practical tools. This mindset is crucial in preventing executive burnout and maintaining a sense of balance.

Tangie used to believe that multitasking is a way to get more done in less time. However, studies have shown that our brains are not wired to handle multiple tasks simultaneously. Instead, multitasking often leads to mistakes and reduces overall productivity.

The Perception of Multitasking as Effective

Despite the evidence against multitasking, many people still believe it is an effective way to manage their workload. This perception stems from several factors:

First, the illusion of productivity plays a significant role. When individuals switch rapidly between tasks, it can feel like they are accomplishing more in a shorter time. Each completed task, no matter how minor, provides a dopamine hit, giving a false sense of efficiency and progress.

Second, cultural expectations and workplace norms often glorify the idea of being constantly busy. In many professional environments, multitasking is seen as a necessary skill for high performers. Colleagues and supervisors may expect fast responses and immediate availability, reinforcing the habit of juggling multiple tasks at once.

Third, technological advancements contribute to this belief. With the advent of smartphones, email, and instant messaging, the lines between different tasks have blurred. The ability to handle communications, work on documents, and manage schedules simultaneously creates the impression that multitasking is not only possible but also essential in our digital age.

Finally, lack of awareness about the cognitive costs is a crucial factor. Many people are simply unaware of the mental strain multitasking imposes. They might not realize that switching tasks depletes mental energy and reduces overall cognitive performance, leading to more errors and lower-quality outcomes.

In summary, the perceived effectiveness of multitasking is driven by a combination of psychological gratification, societal pressures, technological conveniences, and cognitive misconceptions. Recognizing these factors can help individuals understand why multitasking is not the productivity booster it appears to be.

For those looking to break the multitasking habit, here's a refresher of practical tips:

Single-tasking: Focus on one task at a time, giving it your undivided attention. This is also described as approaching tasks one-mindfully.

Eliminate distractions: Turn off notifications and find a quiet workspace to minimize interruptions.

Prioritize tasks: Use the Priority Matrix to identify which tasks need immediate attention and which can be deferred.

Take breaks: Schedule short breaks between tasks to recharge your mental energy and avoid burnout.

Practice mindfulness: You've heard this before. Be present in each task, rather than thinking about what's next.

To illustrate the benefits of single-tasking, consider these scenarios:

During Meetings: Focus solely on the discussion at hand instead of checking emails.

Writing Reports: Allocate uninterrupted time to draft reports, allowing for deeper thinking and better-quality output.

Personal Time: When spending time with family or engaging in hobbies, be present and undistracted.

Single-tasking and mindfulness are intrinsically connected, both focusing on the importance of being present and fully engaged in the current moment. In single-tasking, the emphasis is on dedicating your complete attention to just one task at a time, which naturally aligns with the principles of mindfulness. Mindfulness involves a heightened state of awareness and intentional focus on the present, without distraction or judgment. By adopting a single-tasking approach, you inherently practice mindfulness, as you consciously choose to set aside other distractions and immerse yourself in the task at hand.

This mindful approach to work can significantly enhance the quality of your output, as it allows for deeper concentration and more thoughtful engagement with the task. The cognitive clarity achieved through single-tasking and mindfulness can lead to reduced stress and increased satisfaction, as you are less likely to feel overwhelmed by competing demands. Therefore, integrating mindfulness into single-tasking not only improves productivity but also fosters a more balanced and fulfilling professional life.

Multitasking can unintentionally pave the way for procrastination among busy professionals. When we attempt to juggle multiple tasks at once, our focus is fragmented, leading to a decrease in the quality of attention given to any single task. This scattered focus can result in subpar performance and a lack of meaningful progress, causing tasks to feel overwhelming or unmanageable. Perceiving tasks as daunting brings about feelings of stress and anxiety, which can further deter individuals from taking decisive action — a classic scenario of procrastination.

Additionally, constantly switching between tasks consumes valuable cognitive energy and time, known as "task-switching costs." This not only makes it harder to maintain momentum but also contributes to mental fatigue. As a result, professionals may find themselves postponing important tasks in favor of less demanding or more immediately gratifying activities. Over time, this habit can trap them in a cycle of procrastination, eroding productivity and fostering a counterproductive work pattern.

Moreover, a busy professional environment often demands high levels of attention to detail and swift decision-making. When multitasking becomes a norm, the executive may delay essential tasks, falsely believing that they will handle them more effectively at a later time when they are "less busy."

Unfortunately, that "later time" rarely comes, and the delayed tasks accumulate, creating a backlog that can be daunting to address. Through these mechanisms, multitasking fosters procrastination, undermining the efficiency and effectiveness of professionals who require optimal performance the most.

The Journey from Inherent Skills to Proficiency

Tangie's skills have not come naturally; they are the result of deliberate practice and continuous improvement. Her story serves as a testament to the fact that balance can be learned and mastered over time.

The Impact of Boundary-Setting

Setting boundaries has had a profoundly positive impact on Tangie's life. Before she started being intentional about her time and boundaries, her life was hectic and chaotic. Simple changes, like setting an out-of-office reply during vacations, had a significant impact on her mental well-being. These boundaries allowed her to relax and trust that her team could handle responsibilities in her absence.

Real-life Examples from Tangie's Experience:

Out-of-Office Replies: This simple tool helped reduce the stress of checking emails during vacations.

Communicating Vacation Plans: Ensuring her team knew she was out, which allowed them to take more ownership and make decisions in her absence.

Advice for Fellow Professionals

Tangie's parting advice is to learn and implement these balancing tools early. By identifying what works for you and practicing it consistently, you can avoid the pitfalls of burnout. She likens this process to compound interest – starting small but growing significantly over time.

Tangie's Key Advice:

Start Early: Identify and implement your balancing tools as soon as possible.

Continuous Practice: Keep practicing and refining your approach.

Gradual Improvement: Even small, incremental improvements can have a significant impact over time. Remember, my suggestion is an intentional, daily 1% change. Often high performers want rapid change; however, the real genius is in simplicity, consistency, commitment, discipline, and endurance.

Part of what keeps me balanced is ongoing growth and routine. As we wrap up the A.R.T. of Balance, I would like to share a list of books with you which have greatly influenced my growth, success, and work-life balance. The question "what are you reading" is easily my favorite conversation starter. Scan the Balance Blueprint for a list of books that influenced my journey.

Balance Blueprint

Conclusion

The prefix "auth" in Greek means "self." More specifically, to operate on one's own behalf. Your true self -- devoid of doubt, other people's opinions, and the fear of being left out or otherized. True authenticity is operating in the assurance that you are already enough. There's only one you. A true masterpiece. Fearfully and wonderfully made.

Showing up as your authentic self in every situation is the gateway to true happiness and fulfillment -- fostering confidence, improving resilience, and improving relationships.

Rest is productive. Rest is work. Rest is mandated. Rest is an underutilized superpower. I am able to do all the things I do because I am strategic about rest. You've heard all the cliches from hustle culture scoffing at the thought of rest when in reality rest is a key component of your overall health and well-being. Be intentional and uncompromising about allowing yourself to do absolutely nothing.

Time is your most valuable resource. Use it wisely. Say NO to things you don't want to do -- unapologetically. It's literally that simple. As stated earlier, there's genius in simplicity.

Throughout this book, we've explored the profound impact of living authentically, the necessity of rest, and the critical importance of time consciousness.

In a world that's constantly trying to shape us into something we're not, maintaining your true self, free from doubt, external opinions, and the fear of exclusion, is the gateway to true happiness and fulfillment.

Authenticity

Authenticity cultivates confidence, enhances resilience, and improves relationships. By showing up as your authentic self in every situation, you are not only honoring your unique existence but also setting an example for others to do the same. There's only one you. And that uniqueness is your greatest strength.

Relentless Rest

If there's one mantra to take away from this book, it's this: Rest is productive. We live in a culture that glorifies the hustle and stigmatizes rest, but the reality is quite the opposite. True productivity and creativity flourish when you allow yourself to rest. Be intentional and uncompromising about giving yourself the space to do absolutely nothing. Rest is not a luxury; it's a necessity for overall health and well-being.

Time Consciousness

Time is your most valuable resource. Unlike money, once it's gone, you can't get it back. Therefore, it's imperative to use it wisely. Learn to say NO to things that don't align with your goals or bring you joy, and do so unapologetically. By taking control of your time, you empower yourself to focus on what truly matters.

Done, What's Next

As we conclude, I leave you with a question that encapsulates the essence of this book. Are you willing to commit to a daily 1% shift in order to truly have it all? This small, consistent effort can lead to monumental changes over time. It's possible. I've been there, and I've written this book to guide you through your own transformation.

If you've reached this point and you're thinking, "That was so good, I need more," no worries. Simply go to bonus.artofbalancebook.com for the course.

Remember, true authenticity, purposeful rest, and intentional time consciousness are not just concepts to ponder but practices to integrate into your daily life. By doing so, you set the stage for a life that's not only successful but genuinely fulfilling. The choice is yours. Will you take the first step?

Thank you for allowing me to be part of your journey. Here's to living authentically, resting deliberately, and owning your time. You have everything you need to succeed, and the world is waiting for you to show up as your true self.

It's time to own your authenticity, embrace rest, and take control of your time – because you deserve nothing less than to live out loud as the best version of yourself. You are already enough. You are worthy. And you deserve to truly have it all.

End Notes

Nunes, J. C., Ordanini, A., & Giambastiani, G. (2021). The concept of authenticity: What it means to consumers. Journal of Marketing, 85(4), 1–20. https://doi.org/10.1177/0022242921997081

Reddy OC, van der Werf YD. The Sleeping Brain: Harnessing the Power of the Glymphatic System through Lifestyle Choices. Brain Sci. 2020 Nov 17;10(11):868. doi: 10.3390/brainsci10110868. PMID: 33212927; PMCID: PMC7698404.

Made in the USA
Columbia, SC
30 October 2024

45263448R20080